The
Lewis and Clark
Journals

E.J. CARTER

Heinemann Library
Chicago, Illinois

Designed by Herman Adler Design
Photo research by Bill Broyles
Printed and bound in the United States by Lake Book Manufacturing, Inc.

08 07 06 05 04
10 9 8 7 6 5 4 3 2 1

Library of Congress Cataloging-in-Publication Data
Carter, E. J., 1971-
   The Lewis and Clark journals / E.J. Carter.
      p. cm. -- (Historical documents)
Summary: Provides a history of Lewis and Clark Expedition, including excerpts from journals that Lewis and Clark kept during the journey, and describes how historical documents such as these can be restored and preserved.
Includes bibliographical references (p.) and index.
   ISBN 1-4034-0805-X -- ISBN 1-4034-3433-6 (pbk.)
   1. Lewis and Clark Expedition (1804-1806)--Juvenile literature. 2. West (U.S.)--Discovery and exploration--Juvenile literature. 3. West (U.S.)--Description and travel--Juvenile literature. 4. Lewis, Meriwether, 1774-1809--Diaries--Juvenile literature. 5. Clark, William, 1770-1838--Diaries--Juvenile literature. 6. Explorers--West (U.S.)--Diaries--Juvenile literature. [1. Lewis and Clark Expedition (1804-1806) 2. West (U.S.)--Discovery and exploration. 3. Lewis, Meriwether, 1774-1809--Diaries. 4. Clark, William, 1770-1838--Diaries.
5. Explorers--Diaries. 6. Diaries.] I. Title. II. Historical documents
(Heinemann Library (Firm))
   F592.7.C36 2003
   917.804'2'0922--dc21
                           2003008194

Acknowledgments
The author and publisher are grateful to the following for permission to reproduce copyright material:

Cover photographs by (portraits) Independence National Historical Park; (journals, T-B) David Schultz/Missouri Historical Society, American Philosophical Society; (title bar) Corbis.

Title page, pp. 9, 23 David Schultz/Missouri Historical Society; pp. 4, 5 New York Public Library/Art Resource, NY; pp. 6, 22t, 24, 30B, 32t, 41, 42, 45 American Philosophical Society; pp. 7, 15b, 22b, 30t, 32t, 35, 40, 44 North Wind Picture Archives; pp. 8, 16b, 25, 39 Library of Congress; pp. 10, 14, 29 National Portrait Gallery, Smithsonian Institution/Art Resource, NY; pp. 11, 19 Missouri Historical Society; p. 13t Austrian Archives/Corbis; p. 13b Erich Lessing/Art Resource, NY; p. 15t Edward Owen/Monticello/Thomas Jefferson Foundation; pp. 16t, 18 Independence National Historical Park; pp. 20, 27t, 33b Smithsonian American Art Museum, Washington, DC/Art Resource, NY; pp. 21, 38 Hulton Archive/Getty Images; p. 26 Oregon Historical Society, Portland; p. 27b Bettmann/Corbis; p. 28 Jan Butchofsky-Houser/Corbis; p. 31 Lowell Georgia/Corbis; p. 34 Annie Griffiths Belt/Corbis; p. 36 National Archives and Records Administration; p. 37 Corbis; p. 43 Evan Vucci/AP Wide World Photo.

Special thanks to Derek Shouba for his help in the preparation of this book.

Every effort has been made to contact copyright holders of any material reproduced in this book. Any omissions will be rectified in subsequent printings if notice is given to the publisher.

Some words are shown in bold, **like this.** You can find out what they mean by looking in the glossary.

Contents

Recording Important Events 4

The American Philosophical Society 6

The Unknown West 8

Early Expeditions 10

The $16 Million Bargain 12

Thomas Jefferson and the Enlightenment 14

Captain Meriwether Lewis 16

Captain William Clark 18

Why They Wrote 20

What They Wrote 22

Leaving St. Louis 24

A Cold Winter 26

The Three Forks 28

Great Joy in Camp 30

Studying Native American Life 32

Homecoming 34

Writer's Block 36

Lewis and Clark Rediscovered 38

An APS Archivist 40

Preserving the Journals 42

Anniversary Celebrations 44

Glossary 46

More Books to Read 47

Index 48

Recording Important Events

Throughout history, people have created documents so they will have a record of an important event. Documents may tell stories about how people lived, how significant discoveries were made, or what occurred during a war.

Documents that provide a historical record of something can be divided into two categories: **primary sources** and **secondary sources.**

Primary sources

When historians are studying what happened in the past, they prefer to use primary sources. This term refers to documents that provide a firsthand account of an event. Primary sources can include letters, diaries, newspaper articles, **pamphlets,** and other papers that were written by people who witnessed or were directly involved in an event.

Primary sources can also include official papers that were carefully planned, often with much discussion and argument. The people involved in planning and writing these papers were careful to make

Herds of bison and elk, as shown in this nineteenth-century painting, would have been a familiar site to Lewis and Clark during their travels along the Missouri River.

This painting shows Fort Pierre, on the upper Missouri River. Forts like this were home to the Lewis and Clark expedition during their travels west.

sure the words that went into the documents expressed exactly the thoughts and ideas they wanted them to. Official papers are a clear record of just what the authors intended to say.

Primary sources tell us, in the words of the people who lived during that time, what really happened. They are a kind of direct communication that has not been filtered through a lot of sources. Often, stories that are passed verbally from person to person change as they are told and retold. Facts become muddled and confused, and information is added or left out. Soon, the original story has completely changed.

This is why primary sources are important. Over time, facts can be changed or twisted, accidentally or on purpose, so unwritten accounts of what happened in the past can be incorrect. To find out what really happened and why, historians need to rely on printed or handwritten primary sources.

Secondary sources

Secondary sources are accounts of events written by people who have studied primary sources. They read letters, journals, and other firsthand accounts, then write their own version based on their research.

The American Philosophical Society

The original copies of the journals of Lewis and Clark are stored at the American Philosophical Society in Philadelphia, Pennsylvania. Since the beginning of American history, the American Philosophical Society (APS) has encouraged the pursuit of knowledge. It has **funded** the work of many important scientists and researchers. In fact, many past members of the APS gave advice and support to the Lewis and Clark expedition. Several years after Lewis and Clark returned from their journey, their journals were given to the APS by Thomas Jefferson. For many years those journals were preserved in its library, until **scholars** rediscovered them and made them available to the public.

The APS was **founded** in 1743 to promote the gathering of knowledge in America. Benjamin Franklin played a big role in creating it, and many of the founding fathers were members, including George Washington, John Adams, Thomas Jefferson, Alexander Hamilton, and Thomas Paine. Its building was first located in Independence Square, next to the seat of government at the time. This shows how highly early Americans valued learning and science.

The American Philosophical Society building in Philadelphia has changed little since it was first built in the late 1780s.

The APS still supports research today in fields like eighteenth-century natural history, the study of Native American language and culture, computer development, and medicine. Its library contains 300,000 books and **periodicals,** 100,000 images, and 8 million **manuscripts.** Among the books are famous first edition works by Isaac Newton and Charles Darwin, and part of Benjamin Franklin's personal library. The APS also holds important scientific conferences each year.

The journals of Lewis and Clark

The journals of Lewis and Clark not only tell the story of a journey through the West by two Americans, but they also contain endless amounts of information about what the men found. In the journals, Lewis and Clark describe the birds, fish, animals, and plants they discovered. They talk about the Native Americans they met and describe their customs, languages, and characteristics. They also discuss the rivers, mountains, valleys, cliffs, and waterfalls they encountered in their trip across the country. The journals of Lewis and Clark contain all kinds of interesting facts. The journals, like many **primary sources,** show us what things were like before they were put into museums, out of their natural surroundings.

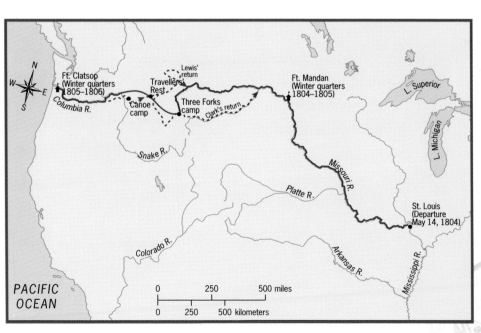

This map shows the route Lewis and Clark traveled. Most of the time, they traveled along rivers.

The Unknown West

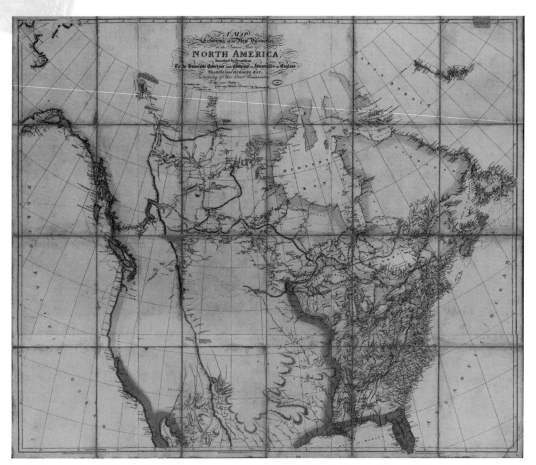

This map of North America was created in 1795. It shows how little was known about the American West at the time.

It is hard to imagine how brave Meriwether Lewis and William Clark were. When they set off on their journey through the American West in 1804, very little was known about the huge mass of land west of the Mississippi River. America was barely fifteen years old. It was just beginning to recover from the **Revolutionary War,** which made it an independent country.

The U.S. government asked Lewis and Clark to explore the western **territories,** but they had no idea what they would find. For all they knew, the land might be inhabited by man-eating animals, poisonous plants, and mysterious diseases. They did know that numerous Native Americans lived in the area, but they did not know whether they were friendly or hostile. They also knew it would be cold in the winter and that it would be hard to find enough food to eat. Despite all this, Lewis, Clark, and less than 50 men set off on one of the most exciting adventures in American history.

Keeping a record

As they traveled, Lewis and Clark kept records of what they saw and experienced. These journals can be read today in their original form and they provide a glimpse of a world that disappeared a long time ago. The journals are one of the most important travel documents ever written. Studying them is one of the best ways to get to know what America was like before Europeans began to inhabit it. The journals also tell us much about the lifestyles of the Native Americans who already lived there.

The actual journals

The Lewis and Clark journals consist of eighteen small notebooks, about 4 x 6 inches (10 x 15 centimeters) large. Thirteen of the notebooks are bound in red **morocco** leather; one is bound in plain brown leather; and four are bound in paper-covered board. In addition to the notebooks, there are also several loose pages and rough notes.

Early Expeditions

Lewis and Clark were not the first people to explore the American West. Numerous nations of Native Americans had lived in the area for centuries and European travelers and **traders** had interacted with them for many years. Fur trading was especially common in these areas, and much of the knowledge about the West came from fur traders. Fur traders often knew how to get from place to place, and had learned to speak one or more Native American languages. However, their knowledge was very limited, and often they lacked the scientific expertise to describe the plants, animals, and geography of the lands they traveled through.

Before Lewis and Clark, several attempts had been made to organize a large expedition that would reveal the land and people west of the Mississippi River. In 1783, a group of Americans including Thomas Jefferson tried to organize a team to explore the west. It was to be led by George Rogers Clark, William Clark's older brother. George Rogers Clark, however, was unwilling to undertake such a journey and the plans fell apart.

George Rogers Clark

George Rogers Clark was a **Revolutionary War** general and was known as the "conqueror of the Northwest." He was living in Kentucky when the American Revolution began, and he organized the local settlers to fight against the British. Clark believed that if two British trading posts at Vincennes and Kaskaskia could be captured, the Americans would be much stronger in that region. In 1777, he led 175 men and easily captured both towns. Thanks to his work, British power south of Detroit, Michigan, was eliminated for the remainder of the war.

In 1786, Jefferson met with John Ledyard in Paris and persuaded him to explore the West. Unfortunately he was arrested by the Russian government before he could reach America. An American General, Josiah Harmer, traveled up the Missouri River in a canoe in 1789, but did not make it very far. In 1792, the American Philosophical Society tried to **fund** a trip by a French **botanist** named André Michaux to gather scientific data. Surprisingly, Michaux turned out to be a French Revolutionary agent, sent to spy on the United States. By the year 1800, many people, especially Jefferson, were anxious to explore the West and find a passage to the Pacific Ocean.

Josiah Harmer

Josiah Harmer was a general in the U.S. army. He also suffered one of the worst military defeats in the Ohio **territory.** In 1787, while dealing with tensions with Native Americans in the Ohio territory, Harmer accidentally led nearly 1,500 men into an ambush. Most soldiers fled, but 182 were killed or missing. The defeat slowed American settlement in the Ohio territory for years. The U.S. army **court-martialed** Harmer for his actions during the ambush. He was found not guilty, but retired soon after.

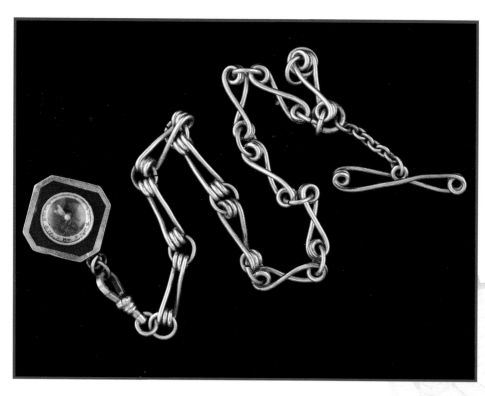

William Clark used this compass during the expedition west. It is now displayed at the Missouri Historical Society.

The $16 Million Bargain

The event that made the Lewis and Clark expedition possible, and even necessary according to many, was the Louisiana Purchase. The Louisiana **territory** was much larger than the state of Louisiana today. It was a gigantic piece of land, as large as the entire United States at that time. It included much of the Great Plains and Rocky Mountain areas, including what are now the states of Arkansas, Missouri, Oklahoma, Iowa, Kansas, Nebraska, South Dakota, Colorado, and Montana.

The French sell the Louisiana territory

The Louisiana territory was owned by Spain for most of the eighteenth century, but in 1800 Spain gave it to France. Since 1789, France had been involved in a **revolution** that led to war with several European powers. The British controlled the most profitable trade with the Native Americans. So neither the Spanish nor the French profited very much from owning the territory.

In 1803, the Louisiana Purchase doubled the size of the United States.

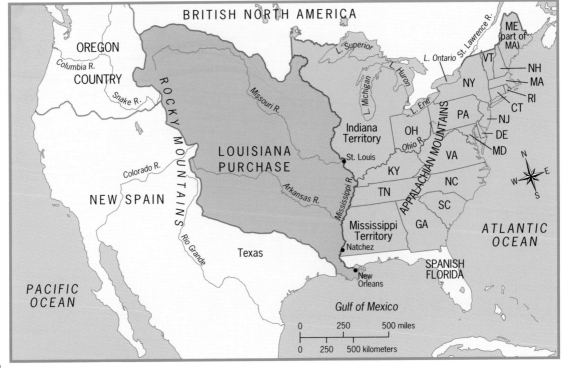

Napoleon Bonaparte

Napoleon Bonaparte was one of history's greatest military leaders. He was born in Corsica in 1769 and became a general at a very young age. Winning battles in Italy and Egypt made him popular with the French people. He declared himself emperor in 1804, but his dream was to spread the French Revolution to the rest of Europe. He frequently declared war on France's neighbors. That is why he sold the Louisiana territory to the United States in 1803—he was planning to declare war on Great Britain as soon as he could raise some money.

In 1799, Napoleon Bonaparte, a successful French general, took power in France. Because his government needed money and the friendship of the United States, he was willing to sell the entire Louisiana territory for only sixteen million dollars in 1803. This was an incredibly cheap price for so much land, and the U.S. accepted right away.

Buying the Louisiana territory gave the U.S. government a new reason to organize an expedition to explore the West. Since the British controlled Canada and might try to occupy the West, the United States needed to stake its claim to the area as quickly as possible.

The Louisiana Purchase **Treaty** was signed on April 30, 1803.

Thomas Jefferson and the Enlightenment

The driving force behind the Lewis and Clark expedition was Thomas Jefferson. Jefferson had dreamed of a voyage through the West for decades, and he made several attempts to organize one. There were many reasons for his interest in the West. Jefferson was a representative of the **Enlightenment**—a believer in the progress of science and reason and the gathering of knowledge.

Thomas Jefferson was an accomplished scientist who made several inventions. He was curious about the plant and animal life of the West,

Thomas Jefferson

Jefferson was born in 1743 in Virginia. As a child he had private **tutors,** and in 1762 he graduated from the College of William and Mary in Williamsburg, Virginia. Jefferson went on to study law and became a lawyer in 1767. In 1769, Jefferson was elected to the Virginia **legislature.** He became Virginia's governor after the **colony** became a free and independent state, and later he was a **diplomat** and the U.S. minister to France. Jefferson was **secretary of state** under President George Washington and vice president under John Adams. He then went on to be president, serving two **terms,** from 1801 to 1809. He retired in 1809 and led an active life. In 1819, he **founded** the University of Virginia. On July 4, 1826, he died at the age of 83.

and hoped it might be economically useful. He also had a lifelong interest in Native American languages and vocabularies, and hoped to add words and phrases to his collection. Most of all, he wanted to have good maps of the West to aid travelers and **traders**.

A route to Asia

There were also political reasons for Jefferson's support for the expedition. Jefferson believed that Lewis and Clark might be able to find a single river that would take them all the way to the Pacific Ocean. If they could do that, ships could sail directly through the United States to countries in Asia like Japan, China, and India. Ships would no longer have to go around the tip of South America in order to travel from the United States to Asia. If the Americans could find this route before the British, Jefferson believed it would give them a strong economic advantage, and ensure that Americans would **colonize** the West rather than the British.

Upon their return, Lewis and Clark presented Jefferson with a pair of elk antlers. Jefferson proudly displayed the antlers at his home in Virginia, called Monticello.

A prairie dog would have been one of the many animals that Lewis and Clark encountered.

Captain Meriwether Lewis

The man Jefferson chose to lead the expedition west was Meriwether Lewis. Lewis was born in 1774 in Virginia. He joined the U.S. army in 1794 and became an officer. He spent a lot of time fighting with and against Native Americans along America's **western frontier.** His family was well known in Virginia, and he became friends with Thomas Jefferson. In 1801, after he had been elected president, Jefferson asked Lewis to be his personal secretary in Washington.

Below is a map that Lewis and Clark used during their expedition. Look closely to see notations made by Lewis in brown ink.

Almost immediately, Jefferson began to think that Lewis would be the ideal person to lead an expedition to the West. Not only did Lewis already possess some knowledge of the West, but he also had experience in living outdoors and leading men. In addition, Lewis had a passion for **zoology** and **botany.** Although he left school at the age of eighteen, he kept studying and had a strong understanding of science.

In 1803, after the Louisiana Purchase was complete, Lewis began to prepare for the expedition. At the same time, Jefferson tried to get **Congressional** approval and **funding** for the trip. Lewis was **tutored** in map-making and received scientific training from some of the nation's top scientists.

Antoine Saugrain

Antoine Saugrain was a doctor in St. Louis, Missouri, who liked to invent things. While waiting to depart on their journey, Lewis and Clark asked him to help provide some items for the expedition. One of the items was a mercury thermometer, so that they could measure temperatures in the West. Saugrain also invented a friction match nearly twenty years before they were widely used. He placed a small amount of sulfur on a piece of wood and then put on a layer of phosphorus. The Native Americans Lewis and Clark encountered were amazed at how quickly they could make fire with these matches.

Lewis always earned the respect and trust of the men he led on the expedition. He was not as warm and friendly as Clark, but he was extremely talented. He showed great courage when the expedition faced dangers, and he could put up with a good deal of physical suffering. He was also an excellent **scholar** with a great eye for detail. Finally, he was a much better speller than Clark!

Captain William Clark

William Clark's life story is fairly similar to that of Lewis. He too was born in Virginia, four years before Lewis. He later moved to Kentucky and served in the army. At one point he was Lewis's commanding officer. Clark occasionally fought against Native Americans and became an accomplished **diplomat.** He knew how to make compromises and peace **treaties** to end fighting. In 1796, Clark left the army and moved to Louisville, Kentucky, where he opened a supply goods store.

Suddenly, in 1803, he received a letter from his old friend Lewis. The letter informed him of the expedition to the West and asked him to be co-leader. Lewis wanted Clark not only for his leadership, but also for his great skills as a **cartographer,** or map maker. One of the greatest achievements of the expedition was the incredible map of the West that Clark made.

A secret Captain

The U.S. army gave Lewis the title of captain for the expedition and he asked that the same rank be given to Clark. The army, however, would only make Clark a second lieutenant. This was very embarrassing, especially since Clark had once been Lewis's superior. So the two leaders decided to keep this a secret. Throughout the expedition Clark was called captain, just like Lewis.

Clark used this elkskin-bound field journal to take notes during the expedition. The elkskin helped protect the notes inside, insuring that they reached home in good condition.

Even though they were together every single day for three years, and their journals fill thousands of pages, there is no sign of a single argument between Lewis and Clark. They had different personalities—Clark was more cheerful and outgoing than Lewis—but they had deep respect for each other. They had no trouble sharing the responsibilities of leadership.

Why They Wrote

On June 20, 1803, Thomas Jefferson wrote Lewis a long letter. He explained exactly what he wanted the expedition to do, and what he hoped it would accomplish. He asked Lewis and Clark to keep a journal recording their observations. In fact, he thought every member of the party should keep a journal. He ordered them to make several copies of their notes so that they were not lost, and to keep them very safe.

Lewis and Clark both made entries in the journal almost every day. They wanted to have two points of view on everything they experienced and saw. That would help make sure that what they observed was accurate.

Sergeant Floyd, a member of the expedition, died on August 20, 1804. He was buried at the top of a bluff near the Missouri River. Amazingly, Sergeant Floyd was the only member of the expedition to die during its course.

Original copies?

There is some argument over when the journals were written. Many people feel that the journals as we see them today in the American Philosophical Society are too neat and clean to be originals. Some historians have even claimed that the journals must have been written later, since they could not have survived such a long journey in such good shape. Most historians, though, have concluded from studying Lewis and Clark's records that they made a first draft in another notebook. Later, they rewrote the entries into a master copy when they had some spare time. Also, the master copies of the journals were preserved in tin boxes and kept very secure. Lewis and Clark knew how important the information the journals contained was, and so they were very careful to keep them clean and dry.

Other journals

Lewis and Clark were not the only members of the expedition who kept journals. Five of the **enlisted** men did as well. Their names were Ordway, Floyd, Gass, Whitehouse, and Frazer. Of these five journals, Frazer's has been lost and Gass's exists only in a printed version. Ordway's journal disappeared for nearly a century, but has been found since then. These journals are not nearly as detailed and interesting as those of Lewis and Clark, but they help add to our knowledge of the journey and some of the people who took part in it.

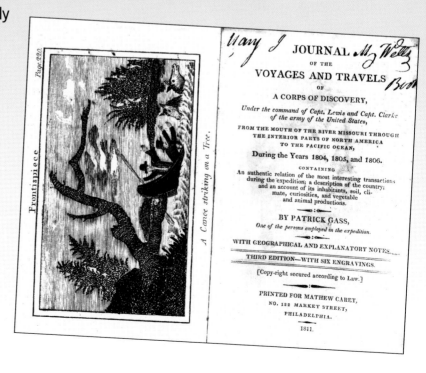

Frontispiece   A Canoe striking on a Tree.   Page 220.

JOURNAL
OF THE
VOYAGES AND TRAVELS
OF
A CORPS OF DISCOVERY,

Under the command of Capt. Lewis and Capt. Clarke of the army of the United States,

FROM THE MOUTH OF THE RIVER MISSOURI THROUGH THE INTERIOR PARTS OF NORTH AMERICA TO THE PACIFIC OCEAN,

During the Years 1804, 1805, and 1806.

CONTAINING

An authentic relation of the most interesting transactions during the expedition; a description of the country; and an account of its inhabitants, soil, climate, curiosities, and vegetable and animal productions.

BY PATRICK GASS,
One of the persons employed in the expedition.

WITH GEOGRAPHICAL AND EXPLANATORY NOTES.

THIRD EDITION—WITH SIX ENGRAVINGS.

[Copy-right secured according to Law.]

PRINTED FOR MATHEW CAREY,
NO. 122 MARKET STREET,
PHILADELPHIA.
1811.

What They Wrote

Lewis and Clark were not writing these journals for their own benefit. The trip was designed to further American national interests. Therefore, Lewis and Clark needed to be able to communicate what they saw and experienced to people back home. But they did not know exactly what those people would be interested in. Therefore, they tried to describe everything. Plants, animals, weather, soil, mountains, and bodies of water were all described in minute detail. When they encountered Native Americans, they described their language, their customs, their style of dress, their diet, their religion, and their hunting methods. Lewis and Clark did not want to leave anything out.

Write what you see

Much of what they wrote came simply from their own observations. At the end of each day, Lewis and Clark recorded what they witnessed. They also tried to interview almost everyone they met—whether they were Native Americans, fur **traders,** or British, French, Spanish, or American **merchants.** They brought along an **interpreter,** George Drouilliard, to help

Below are two pages taken from the journals. Lewis and Clark tried to leave no details out of the journals.

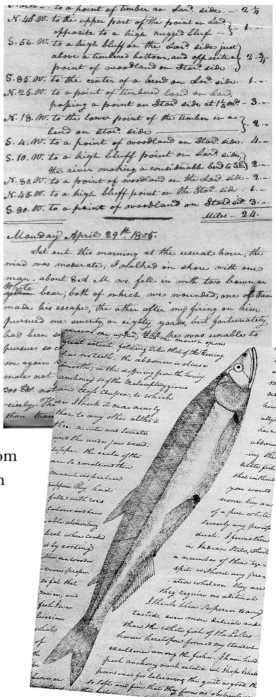

them speak with many Native Americans. In this way, they were able to gather information they would never have noticed on their own.

Multiple purposes

The journals of Lewis and Clark were intended to be many things. On one level, the journals were a travelogue—an account of the trip they made through the West. But the journals were also intended as an advertisement for the West. They invited other adventurers to come explore and perhaps settle in the land. The journals were an effort to describe the Native Americans living in these **territories,** partly so that Americans could live peacefully with them, but also partly so that Americans could control them. Finally, the journals are a scientific log, filled with information useful to scientists. Lewis and Clark were able to put all this data into one very long document.

This telescope, owned by Lewis, is five feet (1.5 meters) long when fully extended. Since this telescope was owned by Lewis, it does not appear on the list of equipment purchased for the expedition.

Leaving St. Louis

After picking up Clark in Louisville, Kentucky, Lewis spent the winter of 1803-04 near St. Louis, Missouri, getting ready for the trip. They gathered supplies for their three boats. The biggest was a keelboat, which could hold up to 27 men. It had a large square sail, and when the wind was not blowing it could be propelled with oars or poles. They had two smaller boats, called pirogues, and several canoes. Many times during the journey the **corps** had to carve new canoes out of large trees after old ones were lost or damaged.

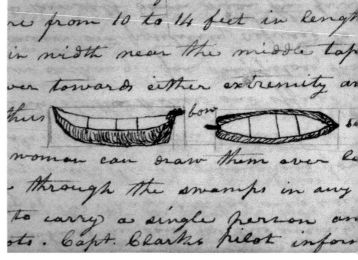

Two views of a canoe were included in the journals on April 6, 1806.

The expedition begins

On May 14, 1804, the party left its camp and began the journey up the Missouri River. Although many of the men taken on the expedition were army soldiers by profession, Lewis and Clark had some problems with discipline when they first left St. Louis. The men were probably excited to be setting off, and maybe a little afraid. On May 17, Lewis wrote in the journal that because some of the men had broken the rules he was "compelled to punish for misconduct." The next day, a **court-martial** was held for William Warner, Hugh Hall, and John Collins. Warner and Hall were charged with staying out all night without permission. They pled guilty and their punishment was 25 lashes with a whip. The punishment was not carried out, however, because they had confessed their guilt. Collins was sentenced to 50 lashes, which he received that evening.

> ### Know It
> The official name of the group led by Lewis and Clark was the Corps of Discovery.

William Warner, Hugh Hall, and John Collins

On May 17, 1804, the following entry was made in the "Orderly Book":

A sergeant and four men of the party destined for the Missouri Expedition will convene at 11 o'clock today . . . and form themselves into a court-martial, to hear and determine (in behalf of the captain), the evidences adduced [brought] against William Warner & Hugh Hall, for being absent last night without leave [permission], contrary to orders; and John Collins, first for being absent without leave; second, for behaving in an unbecoming manner at the ball [party] last night; third, for speaking in a language last night after his return to camp tending to bring into disrespect the orders of the commanding officer.

Deserters

On August 6 Clark wrote, "[w]e have every reason to believe that one man has Deserted—Moses B. Reed." Reed was later captured, punished, and expelled from the corps. A Frenchman named La Liberté also deserted and was never captured. After the first few months, however, the men came to trust Lewis and Clark, and there were no more problems with discipline.

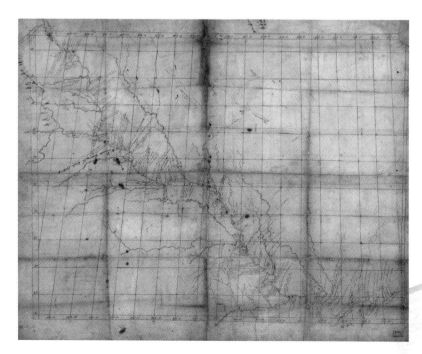

Lewis and Clark used this map on their expedition up the Missouri River. It was created in 1798 and shows the Missouri River and the area from Saint Charles, Missouri, to the Mandan villages of North Dakota.

A Cold Winter

The **corps** made quick progress that summer and fall. One of their goals was to get to know the Native Americans living in the area. They tried to persuade them to declare **allegiance** to the U.S. president, and they distributed flags, peace medals, and other gifts. They had some brief **skirmishes** with the Teton and Sioux Indians near what is now Pierre, South Dakota. Lewis and Clark's quick thinking and the peacefulness of the Tetons prevented any serious violence. By the time winter came, the group had reached Fort Mandan, near Bismarck, North Dakota, where they set up camp.

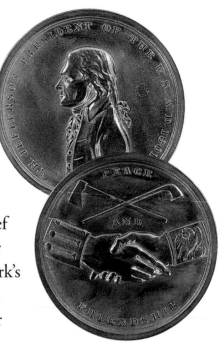

Lewis and Clark handed out Jefferson Indian peace medals during the expedition.

Recording the temperature

It was an extremely cold winter. Thanks to Dr. Saugrain's thermometer, Lewis and Clark could record just how cold it was. Often the journals reported temperatures of -20°F (-29°C), and sometimes -40°F (-40°C). On December 12, 1804, Clark wrote: "the Thermometer at Sun rise Stood at 38° below 0, moderated untill 6 oClock at which time it began to get Colder." The corps spent most of its time trying to find food and keep warm. Several men suffered from **frostbite** during hunting expeditions. Clark wrote on December 8, 1804: "I with 15 men turned out and killed 8 buffalow & one Deer…. This being Cold Several men returned a little frost bit; one of men with his feet badly frost bit."

The Mandan Indians

Relations between Lewis and Clark and the Mandan Indians who lived in the area were very good. On January 16, the journals reported the arrival of 30 Mandans at the camp. Lewis wrote, "we Shot the Air gun,

This painting shows a Mandan village in the late 1830s. Mandan villages would have looked much like this during the time of Lewis and Clark's expedition.

and gave two Shots with the Cannon which pleased them verry much." Lewis' air gun was quite a novelty at the time and impressed everyone who saw it. The Indians were not as bothered by the cold as the soldiers and they were more successful hunters. In return for meat and corn, the corps let them stay in the camp and their blacksmith repaired the Mandans' tools and weapons.

Sacagawea

At Fort Mandan, Lewis and Clark met Toussaint Charboneau, a French **trader** with an Indian wife named Sacagawea. They hired him to be their **interpreter,** since he was familiar with several Native American languages. Charboneau turned out to be a clumsy man who got them into a lot of trouble. But Sacagawea was an extremely brave and resourceful person.

She was a Shoshone Indian and knew the area they would be traveling through in the following year. She helped them **navigate** their way and keep peaceful relations with the Native Americans they encountered further west. What is even more amazing is that she had a baby in Fort Mandan on February 11, 1805. So she not only made this difficult and dangerous journey, but she did it while raising a very young child.

The Three Forks

By spring, the party was ready to resume its journey to the Pacific Ocean. Now they were entering **territory** very few Europeans had seen. They hoped the Missouri River would continue all the way to the Pacific Ocean, but they knew it might not. The party began suffering illness more often and it was harder to find food. By the summer of 1805, they reached the Great Falls, in Montana, and had to **portage** around this giant waterfall.

Concerns surface

They encountered another problem just up the river from the Great Falls. The river forked in three directions, and no one knew which fork to take. Lewis and Clark began to express concern about the rest of the expedition. Lewis knew they were about to enter the Rocky Mountains, and he was afraid they would encounter waterfalls and rapids: "I can scarcely form an idea of a river running to a great extent through such a rough mountainous country without having it's stream interrupted by some difficult and dangerous rapids or falls."

Giant Springs, part of the Great Falls, is considered one of the largest springs in the nation.

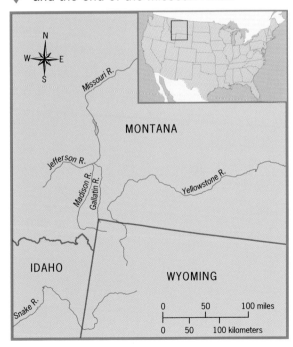

This map shows the three forks area, and the end of the Missouri River.

Albert Gallatin

Albert Gallatin was born in Switzerland in 1761, but came to the United States in 1780. He served in the Pennsylvania **legislature,** U.S. Senate, and House of Representatives before Jefferson appointed him the secretary of the treasury in 1801. As treasury secretary, Gallatin worked to eliminate the national debt.

They also knew they would need horses to get through the mountains and were hoping to meet some Snake Indians, who would trade them horses. Without horses, Lewis wrote on July 27, "the successfull issue [outcome] of our voyage will be very doubtfull or at all events much more difficult in it's accomplishment."

Meanwhile, Clark was feeling very sick with "high fever and aching in my bones." Still, he managed to explore two forks in the river, walking several miles up each of them. Both he and Lewis agreed that they should follow the north fork. Before moving on, they named the three forks after important American leaders: the south fork became Gallatin's River, after the **secretary of the treasury;** the middle fork was named Madison's River, after James Madison; and the north fork was named Jefferson's River.

James Madison

In 1809, James Madison became the fourth president of the United States. Historians called Madison "the father of the Constitution," because the U.S. Constitution is based on his plan. He thought the United States needed a strong national government and worked to convince others of that need. Most of what we know today about the details of the Constitutional Convention comes from the journals he kept.

Great Joy in Camp

After a very difficult passage through the Rocky Mountains on horseback, the **Corps** of Discovery finally reached the Clearwater River in what is now Idaho. The Clearwater led them to the Snake River, and the Snake led them to the Columbia River, which empties into the Pacific Ocean. On November 7, 1805, they knew they were close. Clark wrote in his journal, "[g]reat joy in camp. We are in view of the Ocian [ocean], this great Pacific Octean which we have been So long anxious to See, and the roreing [roaring] or noise made by the waves brakeing on the rockey Shores (as I Suppose) may be heard distictly [distinctly]."

A vote on winter camp

The weather along the coast was very warm, even in November, but also very rainy. Every night they were soaked and several of their canoes filled with water and sunk. The party was "determined to go into Winter quarters as Soon as possible" and they took a vote on where to place the camp. Twelve of them voted to go back up the Columbia River to a drier spot. Nine voted to explore another river,

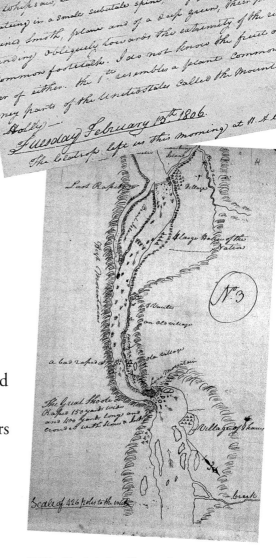

TOP: Sketch by Clark of an evergreen shrub leaf. BOTTOM: Map of the "Great Rapids of the Columbia River, October 30–November 2, 1805."

the Sandy River. And four voted to stay near the Great Falls of the Columbia River. This was a very democratic vote. Clark's slave, York, received a vote and Sacagawea's opinion was recorded as well.

Fort Clatsop

At Fort Clatsop, their new camp, Lewis and Clark had plenty of time to explore the plants and animals of the region. On November 29, Clark "saw a great abundance of fowls, brant, large geese, white brant sandhill Cranes, common blue cranes, cormarants, ravens, crows, gulls, and a great variety of ducks." They found and named many new **species** at this time, and Clark drew dozens of pictures of fish, geese, gulls, vultures, leaves, and pine cones. He also drew objects used by the local Chinook Indians like canoes, hats, knives, tools, and bone fishhooks.

York

William Clark had known York, his slave and personal servant, since they were both children. He brought him along on the expedition and York worked hard at whatever the party needed him to do. He also took care of Clark when he was sick. Clark reported that the Native Americans they encountered were always surprised to see York, because they had never seen an African before. York hoped that after the expedition was finished, Clark would set him free. But it was many years before he was actually freed.

Though the original no longer exists, a **replica** of Fort Clatsop was built at the Fort Clatsop National Memorial in Oregon.

Studying Native American Life

On March 23, 1806, the expedition left Fort Clatsop. They had an easy trip back to the Clearwater River, but then they had to travel again by horseback. Lewis and Clark had left their horses with a group of Nez Perce Indians, led by a chief named Twisted Hair, in what is now Idaho. They spent six weeks waiting to round up their horses and providing medicine to some of the Native Americans.

Healers

When Lewis and Clark had passed through this area on their way to the Pacific Ocean they had distributed medicine to the Nez Perce and had gained a reputation as healers. Men and women flocked to their camp asking for treatment. Many of Lewis and Clark's remedies probably did not work very well, but they tried anyway. It gave them a chance to study Nez Perce life more closely. In May, they spent another month with a group of Nez Perce, waiting for the snow in the Lolo Pass to melt.

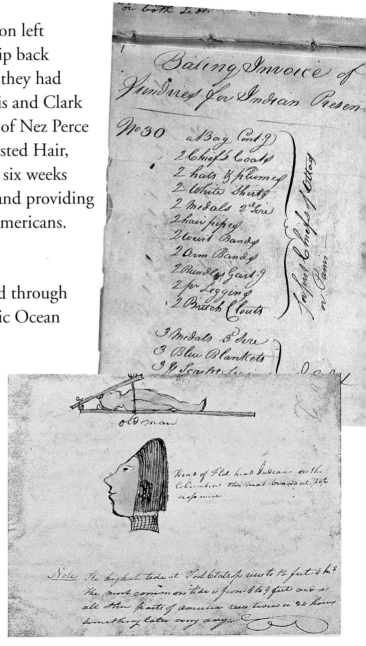

TOP: Lewis's list of Indian presents.
BOTTOM: Clark's sketches of "Flathead" Indians.

These two visits gave Lewis and Clark their best chance to study the lives and habits of the Native Americans living in the West. They tried to record words from Native American languages, since they knew Jefferson would be interested in that. They also examined family and social life among the Native Americans. They described the Native American's clothing in great detail, along with their religion, hunting and fishing techniques, and physical appearance in the journals. Lewis wished he could do more to help those who were sick, but he knew his medicines were not very powerful. On May 18, Clark noted that an old man suffering from "Sore eyes" had visited the camp and was given "eye water." He gave a woman complaining of arthritis "a dose of crème of tartar and flour of Sulphur."

Buffalo hunting

Lewis and Clark both wrote extensively about Native Americans. On May 29, 1805, Lewis wrote about Native American hunting techniques:

Today we passed on the starboard side the remains of a vast many mangled carcases of Buffalow which had been driven over a precipice [cliff] of 120 feet [37 meters] by the Indians…. In this manner, the Indians of the Missouri destroy vast herds of buffaloe at a stroke…. The disguised Indian or decoy has taken care to place himself sufficiently nigh [near] the buffaloe to be noticed by them when they take to flight and running before them they follow him in full speede to the precepice The part of the decoy I am informed is extreamly dangerous, if they are not very fleet [fast] runners the buffaloe tread them under foot and crush them to death….

Homecoming

After the snows melted, Lewis and Clark separated for the first time during the expedition. Clark took some men and Sacagawea and explored the Yellowstone River in what is now Wyoming. Lewis tried to travel up the Marias River, but it was shorter than he expected. He was also shot in the thigh by one of his men who thought he was an elk. The two parties rejoined each other near the Great Falls of the Missouri River. From there the trip home was fairly quick, since they were now traveling downstream.

Lewis and Clark, dead?

Lewis slowly recovered from his injury, but he had to stop writing in the journals. Therefore, only Clark described the final months of the journey. As they neared St. Louis, they began to encounter American

Lewis and Clark most likely would have come across scenes such as this during their travels—bison along the Yellowstone River.

The Marias River (upper left) joins the Missouri River in what is now Montana. This area was the site of a Lewis and Clark campsite.

traders and **frontiersmen.** On September 17, 1806, Clark writes: "this Gentleman informed us that we had been long Since given out [up] by the people of the US Generaly and almost forgotten"—everyone thought they were dead! However, the man also said that President Jefferson still believed they would make it back.

Finally home

It is easy to imagine how excited the men must have been after spending three years away from their homes. As they approached St. Charles, Missouri, on September 20 they "ply [used] their oars very well." On September 23, 1806, they reached St. Louis. Thousands of people came to stand by the river and cheer for them. The next night a local tavern held a great feast for them, and eighteen toasts were read. The final toast went like this: "Captains Lewis and Clark—Their perilous [dangerous] services endear them to every American heart."

The journey home

Lewis and Clark began their journey home on March 3, 1806. They arrived in St. Louis on September 23, 1806, six and a half months later. On that day Clark wrote:
descended to the Mississippi and down that river to St. Louis at which place we arrived about 12 oClock. . . . We were met by all the village and received a hearty welcome from it's inhabitants.

Writer's Block

Upon their return, both Lewis and Clark were awarded 1,600 acres of land on which to settle.

Pursuant to an act of congress passed on the 3d day of March, 1807, entitled "An act making compensation to Messieurs Lewis and Clarke and their companions," Meriwether Lewis is entitled to one thousand six hundred acres of land to be located agreeably to said act, as the option of the holder or possessor, "with any register or registers of the land offices, subsequent to the public sales in such office, on any of the public lands of the United States, lying on the west side of the Mississippi, then and there offered for sale, or may be received at the rate of two dollars per acre, in payment of any such lands."

After arriving home, Lewis planned to write an account of the expedition based on the journals. In the meantime, he was named governor of the Louisiana **territory**. This was a difficult job and it took up much of his time. He also suffered from a serious case of writer's block. He grew ill and depressed, and died in 1809, possibly by suicide. The job of publishing the journals fell to William Clark and Thomas Jefferson. Jefferson retired to his estate, Monticello, in Virginia, after his second **term** as president. Clark became governor of the Missouri territory, a position he held until 1820.

The journals are published

Jefferson and Clark chose two men, Nicholas Biddle and Benjamin Smith Barton, to edit the journals. Barton was a doctor, and he was put in charge of the scientific aspects of the journals. Soon Barton's health began to fail, however, and Biddle took over the entire project himself. Biddle was a 24-year-old lawyer, and knew very little about science. He decided to drop most of the **geological, zoological,** and **botanical** parts from the journals. In 1814, he published a two-volume summary of the journals. This text had great literary value and told an exciting story about the expedition, but the full extent of Lewis and Clark's accomplishments were still not known.

The Biddle edition of the journals was not very successful. Only 1,417 copies were printed and very few were sold. Excitement about their journey had faded and the nation began to forget about Lewis and Clark.

Nicholas Biddle

Nicholas Biddle was born in Philadelphia, Pennsylvania, in 1786. He edited a literary magazine called *Port-Folio*. In 1810 he was elected to the state House of Representatives, where he served one term. Biddle **enlisted** the help of Philadelphia journalist Paul Allen to help him with the Lewis and Clark journals while he was serving in the House of Representatives. Biddle later worked for the Bank of the United States.

Lewis and Clark Rediscovered

Because the American Philosophical Society had helped **fund** the Lewis and Clark expedition, Thomas Jefferson insisted in 1818 that the original copies of the journals be given to them to be stored. For nearly a century after Biddle's edition of the journals appeared, the original **manuscripts** were mostly ignored. Finally, in 1893, a man named Elliot Coues (pronounced COWS), who was a **naturalist,** discovered the original journals. He immediately recognized Lewis and Clark's great scientific gifts and the importance of their journals.

Elliot Coues

Elliot Coues was born in New Hampshire but grew up in Washington D.C. He was **tutored** by an assistant secretary at the Smithsonian Institution. During the **Civil War** he collected **species** of birds, mammals, and reptiles in Arizona. Later, he published a large book on the birds of North America that made him famous among scientists. Coues also fought for equal rights for women. During the last years of his life, he edited not only the journals of Lewis and Clark, but also those of other great explorers of the West, like Zebulon Montgomery Pike, Charles Larpenteur, and Alexander Henry.

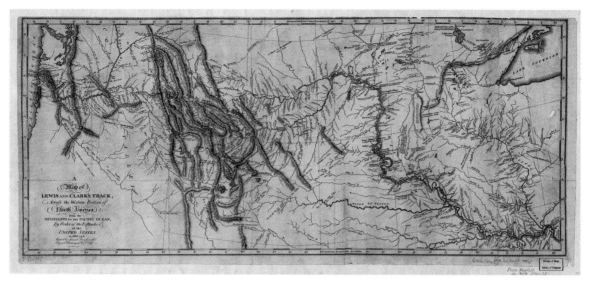

This map of Lewis and Clark's track across the western portion of North America, from the Mississippi River to the Pacific Ocean, was created from an original drawing by Clark.

The journals get republished

Coues decided to republish Biddle's edition of the journals, but with many **footnotes** that tried to fill in some of the gaps. He tried to revive their reputation as important scientists. In 1904–05, a complete edition of the journals was published as well. This was the first time the public could read the actual words of Lewis and Clark as they were originally written. This edition of the journals became a national and an international sensation. Since then, historians and the general public have been fascinated by Lewis and Clark's expedition and the journals that tell its story.

Even more editions

Several other editions of the journals have been published since 1904. In the 1980s, the latest version began to appear, edited by Gary Moulton, and published by the University of Nebraska. This edition is annotated, which means that footnotes have been added by the editor to explain what Lewis and Clark were writing about. It is also much more complete than the 1904 edition, because some new documents concerning the expedition have been discovered since then.

Know It

More than 40 editions of the Lewis and Clark journals have been published. And more are still to come, as historians continue to find new and exciting details about this epic journey.

An APS Archivist

Robert Cox is the head **archivist** of the **manuscript** division at the American Philosophical Society (APS) in Philadelphia, Pennsylvania. This is where most of the Lewis and Clark journals are stored. Cox helps the researchers who work with the documents in the APS collection, and also carries out research projects of his own.

How did you decide to become an archivist?

I've been an archivist for about ten years now, but prior to that I was a **paleontologist.** I moved from paleontologist to historian and archivist. I was always interested in old dead things, so I simply went from old dead animals to old dead manuscripts. It makes sense to me. The APS is a major center for research in the history of science and history of **anthropology,** among other subjects, and it comes in handy that I'm "lucky" to have had formal training in library work, history, **geology,** and biology.

Become an archivist

Interested in history and science? Consider becoming an archivist or document **conservator.** Archivists and document conservators have to be good at working with their hands, because they do detailed work on old documents that must be carefully handled. Some knowledge of science is important, too. Those who do this work must be aware of how different chemicals interact in various environments. Besides working with papers and books, archivists could work with photographs, **textiles,** furniture, and other items.

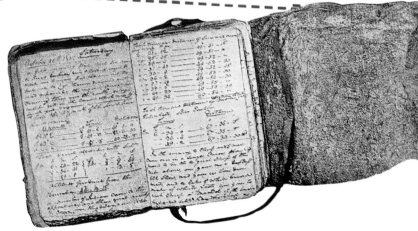

This is one of the many reading rooms in the APS building. Researchers are welcome to come and work on documents that are housed at the APS.

What is your average day like?

On the day-to-day, work here consists of a variety of tasks, ranging from dealing with inquiries [questions] from researchers (either through the mail or e-mail or here in person), scouting for new **acquisitions** for the library, and processing collections to make them available for the public, all the way to talking to groups in the area and doing my own research. We're kept rather busy with requests, researchers, and research.

Preserving the Journals

The Lewis and Clark journals are in very good condition today, although people are allowed to see them only rarely. Thirteen of the journals are bound in red **morocco** leather, and the other five have ordinary leather covers or paper board covers. The paper used by Lewis and Clark was of very high quality, and it is still readable today. The pages have hardly even turned yellow. The journals in their present form are quite easy to read, although Clark's handwriting is much worse than Lewis's!

The journal on the left has a red morocco cover, while the journal on the right is paper board. Both journals, however, are equally legible.

Read the Lewis and Clark journals

The best way to read the journals of Lewis and Clark is in their printed form. Check out the most recent edition of the journals from the University of Nebraska Press. The volumes contain many pages from the original documents. You can also see images of the journals at the APS website, http://www.amphilsoc.org/library/guides/lcills.htm.

Because the American Philosophical Society (APS) wants to preserve the condition of the journals as long as possible, they can only be seen by the public when they go on a traveling exhibition. Most of the time they are stored in acid-free boxes in a high-security room. The temperature in the room is constantly kept at 68°F (20°C), and the **humidity** level at 40-50%. Since they are in boxes, almost no light reaches the journals. Because the paper is of such high quality, the APS's primary concern is to limit the number of people who handle the pages. Their **archivists** do not wear gloves when they touch the **manuscripts** because gloves are more likely to tear the paper.

Upcoming travels

During the **bicentennial** celebrations of the Lewis and Clark expedition, the public will be able to view the journals. The Missouri Historical Society is organizing a traveling exhibition that will include some of the volumes. A couple of journals will also be on display at the American Philosophical Society in Philadelphia, Pennsylvania.

An archivist points to Thomas Jefferson's signature on a confidential message to Congress from January 18, 1803. In the message, Jefferson requests $2,500 for the Lewis and Clark expedition.

Anniversary Celebrations

The Lewis and Clark party left St. Louis, Missouri, on May 14, 1804, and returned on September 23, 1806. That means that in the next few years we will be able to celebrate the 200th anniversary of their trip. Special events are being planned in many places around the country.

For instance, on May 14, 2004, the towns of Hartford and Wood River, Illinois, will celebrate the 200th anniversary of the departure of Lewis and Clark from Camp DuBois. Like many of the special events planned for the **bicentennial,** a **reenactment** of the journey is planned. There will be **replicas** of the boats Lewis and Clark started their journey with, the clothes they wore, and the supplies they carried. The celebration will also include musical and dramatic entertainment, and arts and crafts.

At right is native blue flax (*Linum lewisii*), named for it's discoverer, Meriwether Lewis. Below is a replica of Fort Mandan.

The Lewis and Clark journals are important **primary source** materials that document an epic journey and turning point in American history.

From July 31 to August 3, 2004, Fort Atkinson State Historical Park will recreate a meeting between the **Corps** of Discovery and the Otoe and Missouria Indian tribes. And on Thanksgiving Day 2005, a special Thanksgiving dinner will be held in Chinook, Washington, to remember the decision to spend the winter at Fort Clatsop.

The next few years offer a great opportunity to remember one of the most exciting adventures in American history. By reading the journals of Lewis and Clark, and learning more about their trip across the American West, we are carried back into a past which has disappeared forever.

Anniversary events

You can find a full list of special events being held to honor the 200th anniversary of the Lewis and Clark expedition at http://www.lewisandclark200.org.

Glossary

acquisition something gained by one's own efforts

allegiance loyalty or service to a group, country, or idea

anthropology study of people and their history, development, distribution, and culture

archivist person who works to restore and preserve public records and historical papers

bicentennial 200th anniversary, or its celebration

botanist person who studies plants

botany study of plants

cartographer person who makes maps

Civil War war fought in the United States from 1861 to 1865 between the Union (North) and Confederate (South) states over issues of slavery and states' rights

colonize settle in a new territory that is tied to an established nation

colony settlement in a new territory that is tied to an established nation

Congressional having to do with Congress

conservator person who is responsible for the care, restoration, and repair of documents and other historical artifacts

corps organized branch of a country's military forces

court-martial court of officers for the trial of members of the armed forces or others within it area

diplomat person sent by one government to negotiate with another

Enlightenment time of progress of science and reason through the gathering of knowledge

enlist join the armed forces as a volunteer; to obtain the help of

footnote note at the bottom of a page

found start something, like a school

frontierman person living on the edge of the settled part of a country

frostbite slight freezing of a part of the body

fund provide money for

geology study of the history of the earth and its life, especially as recorded in rocks

humidity amount of moisture, or water, in the air

interpreter person who tells the meaning of; translator

legislature group of elected individuals who make laws for those who elect them

manuscript something written by hand or typewritten

merchant store owner or trader

morocco fine leather made from goatskin

naturalist person who studies nature, especially of plants and animals as they live in nature

navigate travel by water; steer or direct the course of

paleontologist person who studies fossils of extinct plants and animals

pamphlet booklet with no cover, usually made of paper folded into smaller parts

periodical published at regular intervals, such as a magazine

portage carry gear on land

primary source original copy of a journal, letter, newspaper, document, or image

reenactment act or perform again; repeat the actions of an earlier event or incident

replica exact copy

revolution overthrow of one government or ruler and the substitution of another by the governed; rebellion

Revolutionary War American fight for independence from British rule between 1775–1783

scholar student; person who knows a great deal about one or more subjects

secondary source written account of an event by someone who studied a primary source or sources

secretary of state person in the U.S. government who is responsible for foreign affairs

secretary of the treasury person in the U.S. government who is responsible for managing public debt

skirmish minor fight or dispute

species group of plants or animals that is made up of related individuals producing or able to produce young with one another

term period of time fixed by law

territory area belonging to or under the rule of a government

textile item made from woven cloth

trader person who takes part in the exchange, purchase, or sale of goods

treaty agreement, often between countries, arrived at after a negotiation process

tutor person who teaches another

western frontier western-most border of the United States

zoology study of animals and animal life

More Books to Read

Bergen, Lisa Rice. *The Travels of Lewis and Clark.* Chicago: Raintree, 2000.

Bursell, Susan. *The Lewis and Clark Expedition.* Mankato, Minn.: Bridgestone Books, 2002.

Isaacs, Sally Senzell. *The Lewis and Clark Expedition.* Chicago: Heinemann Library, 2003.

Moulton, Gary E. (ed.). *The Lewis and Clark Journals: An American Epic of Discovery.* Lincoln, Neb.: University of Nebraska Press, 2003. An older reader can help you with this book.

Santella, Andrew. *Lewis and Clark.* Danbury, Conn.: Franklin Watts, 2001.

Webster, Christine. *The Lewis and Clark Expedition.* Danbury, Conn.: Children's Press, 2003.

Index

Adams, John 6
American Philosophical Society (APS) 6–7, 11, 21, 38, 40, 41, 43
American West 8, 10, 45
animals 15, 22, 31
archivists 40–41, 43

Barton, Benjamin Smith 37
bicentennial 43, 44–45
Biddle, Nicholas 37, 38, 39
boats 24, 44
Bonaparte, Napoleon 13
botany 17, 37

Camp DuBois 44
Charboneau, Toussaint 27
Chinook Indians 31
Civil War 38
Clark, George Rogers 10
Clearwater River 30, 32
Columbia River 30–31
conservators 40
Corps of Discovery 24, 30, 45
Coues, Elliot 38, 39
court-martials 11, 24, 25

Drouilliard, George 22–23

Enlightenment 14

Floyd, Sergeant 20
Fort Clatsop 31, 32, 45
Fort Mandan 26, 27, 44
Fort Pierre 5
France 12 22
Franklin, Benjamin 6, 7

Gallatin, Albert 29
geology 37, 40
Great Britain 12, 15, 22
Great Falls 28, 34

Hamilton, Alexander 6
Harmer, Josiah 11
homecoming 34–35

Independence Square 6

Jefferson, Thomas 6, 10, 11, 14–15, 16, 17, 20, 29, 35, 36, 38, 43
journal content 7, 9, 20–21, 22–23, 33

Ledyard, John 11
Louisiana Purchase 12, 17
Louisiana territory 12, 13, 36

Madison, James 29
Mandan Indians 26–27
Marias River 34, 35
Michaux, André 11
Mississippi River 8, 10, 20, 39
Missouri Historical Society 11, 43
Missouri River 4, 5, 11, 24, 25, 28, 34, 35
Missouri territory 36
Monticello 15, 36
Moulton, Gary 39

Native Americans 7, 9, 10, 11, 12, 15, 16, 17, 18, 22, 23, 26, 27, 31, 32–33
Nez Perce Indians 32

Ohio territory 11
other journals 21

Pacific Ocean 11, 15, 28, 30, 39
Paine, Thomas 6
Philadelphia, Pennsylvania 6
preserving 42–43
primary sources 4–5, 7, 45
publishing 36–37, 39

Revolutionary War 8
Rocky Mountains 12, 28, 30

Sacagawea 27, 34
Sandy River 30
Saugrain, Antoine 17, 26
secondary sources, 4, 5
Sioux Indians 26
Snake Indians 29
Snake River 30
Spain 12, 22
St. Charles, Missouri 35
St. Louis, Missouri 17, 24, 34–35, 44

Teton Indians 26
three forks 28–29
traders 10, 22, 35

University of Nebraska 39, 43

Washington, George 6
West, the 7, 11, 13, 14–15, 17, 18, 23, 33
western frontier 16
western territories 8

Yellowstone River 34
York 31

zoology 17, 37